Moose

Moose

Jenny Markert

T H E C H I L D ' S W O R L D®, INC.

Library of Congress Cataloging-in-Publication Data

Markert, Jenny.
Moose / by Jenny Markert.
p.   cm.
Includes index.
Summary: Describes the physical characteristics,
behavior, habitat, and life cycle of moose.
ISBN 1-56766-583-7 (alk. paper)
1. Moose—Juvenile literature.
[1. Moose.]   I. Title.
QL737.U55M294   1999
599.65'7—dc21   98-34032
                              CIP
                              AC

Photo Credits

ANIMALS ANIMALS © Leonard Lee Rue III: 19
© 1996 Craig Brandt: cover, 9, 30
© Daniel J. Cox/Natural Exposures, Inc.: 20, 24
© DPA/Dembinsky Photo Assoc. Inc.: 6
© 1998 Michael H. Francis: 26
© 1997 Robin Brandt: 10
© 1998 Robin Brandt: 29
© Tim Davis: 13
© Tom and Pat Leeson: 2, 15
© Tom Bean/Tony Stone Images: 16
© W. Perry Conway: 23

On the cover...

Front cover: This big male moose lives in a national park in Alaska.
Page 2: From close up, you can see this moose's thick fur.

Table of Contents

Imagine that you are walking through a forest on an autumn afternoon. The skies are clear and the air is cool. Birds are chirping, bees are buzzing, and squirrels are collecting nuts for the coming winter. Suddenly, you hear rustling leaves and cracking branches. You take a few steps forward, unsure of what lurks up ahead. As you peek around a tree, you see an enormous creature chomping on a mouthful of leaves. What could this huge animal be? It's a moose!

⇐ This large male moose is eating leaves near a meadow.

What Are Moose?

Moose belong to the same group of animals as deer and elk. They are also **mammals.** Mammals have warm blood and feed their newborn babies milk from their bodies. Monkeys, cows, and people are mammals, too.

Moose are much larger than other types of deer. An adult moose can stand more than seven feet tall. That's taller than most basketball players! They can weigh more than 1,800 pounds, or about the same as 10 full-grown men.

This female moose weighs 1,000 pounds and stands 6 feet tall. ⇒

Many people who see a moose in the wild think it's a funny-looking animal. That's because moose have a long **snout,** or nose, and large, floppy ears. They have long legs, a little tail, and a flap of skin under their chin that looks like an old man's beard. Together, these features make the moose look to some people like a goofy cartoon character.

What Are Antlers?

Moose are best known for the huge bones called **antlers** that grow out of their heads. Only male moose have antlers. Some moose have antlers as long as six feet across. That's as large as a dining room table!

Antlers do not keep growing. Instead, they fall off once a year. Each spring, the male moose begins growing new antlers. The tiny pieces of bone look like little knobs growing out of the moose's head. The little antlers are covered with a soft, furry skin called **velvet.** The velvet contains tiny blood vessels that help the antlers grow.

It is easy to see the fuzzy velvet on this moose's antlers. ⇒

By early autumn, the moose's antlers reach their full size. Slowly, the furry velvet starts to peel off. The moose rubs its antlers against trees and rocks to get rid of the loosening velvet. After the velvet falls off, the antlers are smooth and sharp. They remain with the moose until the middle of winter, when they finally become brittle and break off.

The velvet is just starting to peel off this moose's antlers. ⇒

Although moose are common in the forests of the northern United States and Canada, few people ever get to see one. That's because moose are very shy animals and like to be left alone. When they sense that people are near, moose quickly move deeper into the forest. They can smell people from as far away as one mile, and they can hear well, too. So even if you are very quiet, chances are a moose will hear you coming!

⇐ This female moose has moved deep into a forest to stay safe.　　17

How Do Moose Hide?

Even if you do get close to a moose, it will be hard to see. That's because the moose's dark brown color blends in with the colors of the forest and grasses where it lives. Coloring that helps an animal blend in with its surroundings is called **camouflage.** The moose's antlers act as camouflage, too. That's because the antlers look a lot like tree branches.

This male moose is hard to see as it walks through some trees. ⇒

If you are lucky enough to see a moose, you will probably see it eating. Moose spend most of their lives looking for food. Moose are **herbivores,** or plant eaters. They eat things such as leaves, twigs, grasses, and tree bark. In the summer, moose also eat plants that grow underwater, such as water lilies and pond weeds.

⇐ This female moose is eating leaves in a Wyoming forest.

How Do Moose Eat?

In order to eat water plants, moose have to be good swimmers. They can swim for hours without taking a break. Sometimes, moose will even dive deep underwater to find food! They fill their mouths with plants that grow on lake bottoms. Then they swim back to the surface to swallow their meal.

When they are in shallow water, moose simply dip their long snouts underwater to find food. But even when they are eating, moose are always looking out for danger. Their ears remain out of the water to listen for sounds of approaching enemies.

This female moose is feeding in a pond near the Rocky Mountains. ⇒

Moose eat a lot of food. In the summer months, an adult moose may eat 60 pounds of food in a single day. That would be like eating 240 hamburgers! In the winter, food is harder to find. Moose must use their big feet to dig beneath the snow to find grasses and weeds. They also use their wide noses to push snow away from buried plants. Even if they search all day long, they may find only 40 pounds of food.

What Are Baby Moose Like?

When spring arrives, many female moose have babies. A female moose usually has two babies at a time. Baby moose, or **calves,** are about the size of a large dog when they are born. At first, the calves wobble uneasily on their skinny legs. But soon they are strong enough to walk and run. They follow their mother everywhere and learn from her. The calves stay with their mother for up to two years.

Do Moose Have Any Enemies?

Because of their huge size, adult moose do not have many enemies. But wolves and black bears often try to catch young, sick, or old moose to eat for dinner. One of the moose's most dangerous enemies is the grizzly bear. If it is hungry enough, a grizzly will use its sharp teeth and claws to attack even a healthy adult moose.

Moose are well prepared to fight an enemy if they must. Male moose sometimes defend themselves with their sharp antlers. Both males and females use their powerful legs and giant feet to kick and stomp, too. In fact, one strong swipe of a moose's foot can break the back of an enemy.

This bull moose is ready to use its antlers to defend itself. ⟹

Are Moose in Danger?

In the past hundred years, people have begun to move into the northern forests where moose live. As people destroy the forests to build cities and roads, the moose have fewer places to go. There is less food for them to eat and fewer safe places to raise their babies.

To make sure moose are around for a long time, people must begin to save the areas where these animals live. We must learn how to protect our forests and keep them clean. Then one day, maybe you, too, will be able to see one of these shy creatures in the wild.

⇐ This large male moose lives in a national park in Alaska.

Glossary

antlers (ANT-lerz)
Antlers are bones that grow out of an animal's head. Male moose grow very large antlers.

calves (KAVZ)
Calves are baby moose. Calves stay very close to their mothers when they are young.

camouflage (KAM–oo–flazh)
Camouflage is colors or patterns that help an animal hide. Moose use camouflage to blend in with their surroundings.

herbivores (HER–bih–vorz)
Herbivores are animals that eat only plants. Moose are herbivores.

mammals (MA–mullz)
Mammals are animals that have warm blood and feed their babies milk from their bodies. Moose, monkeys, cows, and people are all mammals.

snout (SNOWT)
A snout is another word for a nose. Moose have long, wide snouts.

velvet (VELL–vet)
Velvet is a soft fuzzy skin that covers new antlers. When a moose's velvet dries up, the moose rubs it off on trees and bushes.

Index